T5-CCN-390

Walking Upright

poems by

w. loran smith

Arable Press   Louisville, Kentucky

Copyright © 2005 by w. loran smith

Walking Upright

FIRST EDITION

Printed in the United States of America

All rights reserved.

ISBN 0-9723524-5-7

No part of this book may be reproduced in any mechanical or electronic means without permission in writing from the author, except for short quotes used in reviews.

The black & white photo on the front cover of this book was taken by Keith Auerbach.

Arable Press
514 Washburn Avenue
Louisville KY 40222

DEDICATION

Without the light of my wife, my children, and all my friends at the Chartreuse Table, this book would not have been possible.

Table Of Contents

The Last Confessionalist

If all joy is bundled, like my mother said, into a few shining moments
you hold up to the sun one day near death, all shaky and cloudy-eyed,
sitting on some forlorn velvet couch or pegged chair
hewn and brought across the bible-thick mountains,
something held up and reflecting off the coin silver,
refracting through the crystal goblets no one ever uses.
If all that is true, which I believed when she would tell me,
her cigarette and scotch poised in that Betty Grable stance,
then all my wives are fools who hunkered down and did all
they could to keep a good year going long past its charm.
And what about my children, what will I leave them,
when I look to their smiles, big and bright, for my grain of truth,
when all my past is a wind-up ghost sprung and bouncing off my skull,
what do we do these days with persons like that,
all the old sanitariums grown over with such poetry of death.
And when my fine tweeded contemporary, the professor
(yes, they are still abounding), speaks of spring and roosters
and buttermilk chickens frying in the memory of his pastoral house,
why do I think of that same spring long ago, as my father, enraged,
fifteen years without his wife's bed, banging at his chores
as I go out to the garage, where there are nestings and chirpings
among the bottles in the eaves, and viburnum bushes that have the scent of God
distilled in week-long blossoms and birth is wobbling all around,
in the same land as that professor, same blue sky and same soft sun.
Why then, do I think about bending down to the gas can to take long
meditative breaths of those sweet fumes, then pulling the cord over and over
until I laugh and go careening across the lawn, careening down
the street, careening through the lives of those I tried to say I loved.
What amount of goodness does it take to fill a vessel so full of that.

Where Those Half Breed Sponge Fishermen Go To Die

My old friend Virgil Rankin calls to tell me he finally got
that back disability check. Says, I went mental, baby,
it's the only thing the Feds will spring for anymore.
Says he bought himself a thirty-acre lake near Tarpon Springs.
Got an old glass bottom boat that's scratched and leaks a little,
but you can still see all the way to the bottom.
I got it tricked out like a low rent Disney World.
Give you two bucks off for a needle scar or a yellow pall.
Says right on the sign—No whimpering. No spitting up bile.
Speaking of which—how you doing, Super Star?
He tells me—every morning some rusted Valiant or Caprice
is parked out by the gate. God knows how they find it in the middle of the night.
It rocks, dude. See, nobody figures how I do it, but I got these flaming
heads that pop up when you come gliding through the reeds.
I call them Avarice, Greed, and old Gluttony, it'll scare the shit out of you.
The way they start screaming and catching on fire, floating up
to the boat, begging to be saved, the way we used to do.
Virgil calls me at three thirty in the morning to tell me this.
Says, he wears a monks cowl now, only drinks on weekends.
Says, this could be it, what he's been looking for—the only drawback
is the heat, like that old inferno of a factory we worked in,
you remember that? Ten ton presses, forty-ouncers,
all those half-fingered men? Virgil's Lake of Living Fire
Next Exit, Cheap tours! Free Ice Cream! Alligator wrestling!
Has a good ring to it, don't it Bro?—So, when you coming down?

Then There Is God Throwing You His Tiny Blessings

I have a friend who used to live in a packing carton back of a strip bar downtown.
He had put a blanket in it and a rusty flashlight, a book or two,
and even a little flap in the side that he could raise up to watch for the police,
or the boys from Portland who had wrapped him up once in newspapers
and set them on fire to watch him whirl around in the dark.
He told me that one night as he lay there pissing on himself,
he happened to look out of his little window to see this poor guy
passed out face first in the glass and ballast-stone alley.
Now my friend, who had been living like this for nearly two years,
said he looked out at this poor fellow and made a promise,
right then and there, that if he ever got as pitiful as that,
he would get off the wine and the dope right away. Straighten up his life.
Which is maybe a little what going crazy is like.
I mean, when exactly is that moment when the world stops making sense?
Is it when the voices speak plainly to you, or when you haven't moved in days
while the phone rings and the doorbell screams some imagined terror?
But even then, if you bother to lift up the flap of your brain to look at the world,
to make sure you are alive, there will always be someone a little crazier out in the alley.
Like that girl you knew once, who would flay her skin and sew the pieces
into little purses to keep her poems in. See, it is always a hard call
when you're right in the thick of it. When your skin is itching, and nothing,
not God, or your children, or even poetry can hold back the flood.

Lawnmower

It seems that I am missing something.
Like a filter to mute the voice of the old man
who fixes my lawnmower, telling me how
he killed his three children on Christmas Eve
after drinking a fifth, after his wife begged
him not to take them out for a ride.
My other problem is complete honesty,
because I am in a step group with the old man,
and since there are just so many horrors
like this to go around, I don't have to tell you
about driving on the wrong side of the expressway,
or that creepy guy at the motel whose dingy underwear
I see lying on the bed next to me, at least once a day.
Also, I have never told the old man that no matter
how sweet he is, or how the other members
can call him for comfort any hour of the night,
or that no matter how smooth my lawnmower runs,
there is a part of me that believes only a coward
could wake each day to birds singing, to that greasy garage
full of broken lawnmowers, or even that baby
I heard crying as he talked about the choke,
and the throttle, and how sharp the blade was.

On The Edge

All I ever wanted
Was to be as pure as Shelley's heart.
A moist rose among charred bones.

I thought there would always be songbirds
Weeping honey on my verse.

But then I killed a sea gull in Michigan.
A lucky stone thrown from the beach.

And our crooked creek was damned.
Bulldozers on the banks.

Crows argued outside my window
As I dragged my father from the blue smoke in our garage.
And that girl on the news,
A bloom of flames running naked down her palm-lined street.
Little things like that.
Like Shelley's boy going down to the lake.

I forget exactly.
But it was soon, very soon after that.

Kentucky Dream Time

I'm always wanting gardens of something to bloom my way.
Women, words, shuck beans, milk gravy on my plate,
kids kissing me like lollipops. True love of me,
sometimes the whole shebang of my every living moment.
So when I was driving to the gym last week,
starlings, like grave walkers, sitting in bare-assed maples,
thinking how life's a bitch of a fast ride,
one big roller coaster always going down.
I started dreaming I had game that day.
Had the rocket in my baggy shorts, electrolytes buzzing,
muscles limber, and fingertips tingling.
I started dreaming I had the rock fever, the Kentucky Religion,
the big rim disease. I started believing I had game at forty-seven.
Knowing anywhere I went, any crowd I was squeezed in,
from NYC to Incognito, and all those folks in between,
there weren't a dozen or more farm boys, big shots, fat cats,
gang bangers, brain bats, or pretty boys who could shut me down.
Not even in their dreams, cause I got game,
got me a piece of the rock, momentary fame,
got the white boy finger roll to a liberated science.
I'm half in the zone, like a gong, like a Zen Koan.
You can't figure me out cause I'm in your face, Dog.
Arch so pretty it's like bursting through the Carolina Pines,
and over the hot sand to dive in cool blue ocean time.
The rock….. It's mine. My puppet, my gypsy ball,
spinning this way and that, fast forward like an asteroid
hurtling through space. I mean, It's between the legs time,
over the asphalt time, Appalachian dreams in the dirt
behind the barn, a big blue mountain wildcat with rabies time.
Doctors of dunk operating on you with a diamond tipped drill.
I got the mad hops, feigning left, then breaking you down.
So quick, it'll make you cry, laughing at the orange round joy of being had.

The whole funky world holding its breath, singing Alleluias,
as I lead 'em to the promised land, and for one long arc of a moment,
all the world's troubles fading away. Now you see it,
now you don't. That's right...... I got game, Y'all.

The Short End

Hey, you malcontents, you confessionalists,
you alcoholic fathers roaring through nervous houses.
You bird men in orange jumpsuits,
broom stick lovers whistling past your cell,
I have the bad news no one wants to tell you.
That you and all your problems,
your seven pounds or so of birth were nothing special.
Not even a speck to the weight of the world.
Hardly an amoeba in the fossil beds that eddy up.
See, the mistake is thinking that just because God
has ears about the size of Texas, he can hear you.
That he could see the blue teeth marks on her arms,
or the nurses on their coffee breaks, saying,
"seven more pounds of trouble for the state."
No. You were only the short end of a sticky day,
while your fathers spit in barrels and laughed it off.
In this life, you've got to take what's given you.
Take the dogwood blossoms, fat and burned at the edges.
Take the dogs licking at your fever. Christ in fur.
Take the frightened children when you turn cold.
There are lambs caught in the brambles wherever you go,
and the wolves' eyes on the ridge are mistaken for stars.
You, the curl of fingernail from the world's short memory,
carry your parcel of fear like a precious stone.
One step, then another, then another, and then it's done.

Owl Wise

When I was fourteen,
I was tender for the field
that spread out behind the liquor store.
And girls were smelly blossoms
we'd peek at through windows
etched in the moon. Shy there,
giggling boys, we confessed nothing
and were strong, X-men, Ninjas,
Panthers, running in our wine crazed suits.

When I was fourteen,
vibrations of my joy outweighed
the catacombs of fatherless houses,
their unearthly bruised flickering.
And I could still count the hope of things.
Still turn its golden screw,
the taut wire that held God and me
below the farm tree, safe in its bowl of roots.
Snug and without peril as the clouds raced by
and cry for cry, nothing was impossible.

When I was fourteen,
the cavity in my chest was just a fissure,
My brain still healed itself, Dylan and I,
Sexton and I, Shelley and I went walking
in those fields and lay down with nothing,
and ran our fingers through each other's hair
waiting for our fathers to call us home.
Home, where death ate the grass,
sat at the table and counted the roar
of silence, the dog's low growl.

When I was fourteen,
I thought you outran your fate,

but soon sleep would be my best friend.
The white capped surf of the fan blades
humming low beneath my dreams,
and father, in his bed, was barely breathing.
He was an apple blossom then.
The magnolia buds were all clichés,
drifting fists of heaven through the screen.

I was owl wise then,
Prince of the dawn.
A velvet and satin boy,
King of my future,
and Lord of the stars.

Vega

My dad had the only cream puff Vega that ever rolled off the line at GM, and in a life where everything else was broken, this was his baby, and he liked to tell everybody how he just couldn't figure out why Vegas had this bad reputation and how maybe people just didn't know what to do when it came to a car, you see, maintenance was the key, any idiot knew that, which was, of course, his point, this country being filled with nincompoops, and namby-pambies, sitting around all day with their fingers up their butts, because his little baby ran just fine, thank you, and man, he loved those new fangled aluminum Mags and the custom shifter knob he had to wait six weeks to get, but as much as the old man loved that Vega, he loved his boy even more, and by damn, or by fate, or just to prove him right on the whole way he looked down on this world inhabited by a bunch of sissies and guys without backbones and guys that were going to be left behind if they didn't start building a better foundation, my dad lent me his Vega and waved when we left, like a lover waving to a train as I rode up the street right to the liquor store with the speakers rattling and speed-shifting from first to third, and squealing the tires, squealing all over town until the Rebel Yell kicked in, and while I was getting sort of misty eyed looking over at a White Castle, one of those assholes Dad was always telling me about was stopped in the middle of the road, at a green light of all things, when BAM! I crushed that Vega's engine into half its size, but true to form, this miracle of a car kept on running and so I ran, what with the drinking and police on the way .... I kept on going to bars where my two o'clock girlfriends were sulking in their booths, until coming home around four in the morning, the telephone lines started singing, "turn this way, turn this way," and still flustered by the close call and the way the guy I had hit was rubbing his neck real fake like when he got out, I whipped the steering wheel towards the sound, and that beautiful silver Vega slid left, shimmied a little when I hit the curb, but just kept going right through the pole like it wasn't even there and I was tired then, walked a little ways towards home, and found a car on the way to sleep in, to sleep like the dead in, without a worry, so soundly in fact, it was late morning before this guy was standing there saying, "uh...excuse me, but what in the hell are you doing in my car," so I got out and walked the rest of the way home, to my dad sitting on the couch with two policemen looking real sympathetic towards this man and his no good son, and I think I broke his heart, because there was no fixing the Vega and when Dad saw it, he almost cried. Yeah, I'm pretty sure I broke his heart, which in my defense, wasn't built nearly as sturdy as that Vega's was.

A Swirl Of Smoke Rising From My Ranch House

My neighbor and I are doing that middle aged thing
of talking up our wild days, and I am saying
how ironic it is that the only thing left of it
is deep in the bowels of my computer,
when my artist friend exhales, passes the pipe and says,
well, if I could wish for anything at all,
it would be to live in absolute poverty
like one of Van Gogh's potato eaters,
because I'm tired of dreaming what the rich will want next.
I nod, yes, we men should stick together,
so I would have a hut in the field next to yours,
and at the end of the day, our hands would be raw,
while the moon drenched our fleshy-eyed potatoes.
I would dream of only simple things,
of kindling, and spotted cows, their teats so full,
our children would grow straight and tall.
My artist friend, high as the suburban twilight permits,
says he would be so sure of a Heavenly Father's grace,
that if our children perished with blood spotted lungs,
he'd know for sure that angels would blow their airy souls
across the sky to tumble into God's huge lap.
Then we could share our monthly teaspoons of sugar,
watch as our wives broke open their Christmas oranges,
the meat bursting on grateful, satisfied tongues.
And we would slog through the knee-high mud,
to ring our cow-bells when the bishop's carriage passed,
his jeweled hand waving like honey over bread.
My friend leans back and folds his hands, as I think
about the casket he had just built for his father.
All the lovely hieroglyphs his clan had painted on the sides,
the bagpipes howling to us rows of sleepy mourners.
I think about my own son's moaning yesterday,
the heaving and fluttering of his thin asthmatic chest.

My wife bundling him up, driving to the hospital
while I lay on my daughter's bed, listening to her
snore like a sailor on her twisted cartoon sheets.
All the way there, I hovered above my wife's station wagon,
her night blindness gone with the clear vision of her faith.

And how, for the first time in years, I tried something
so medieval, something so incredibly simple that had been
caught in my throat all these years, this whisper, this hoarse
stone of a prayer to always keep my family warm and safe.

The Rovers Are In Town

A seventeen year-old member of the Rovers, an infamous band of flimflam
artists, confesses to the severe beating of an elderly deaf mute woman in
Louisville, Kentucky.

Any old person can tell about the lush marooning
of days in an old house with the shades drawn down.
How the sun eats time, fades what little you have;
the wall paper, the scratched and ringed furniture,
even your own face in the gold leaf mirror above the desk.
The deaf mute lady down the street knows these things,
and because one of the boys can sign, they are sitting now
on her Duncan Phyfe, three sweating glasses of boiled tea
between them, and yes, she tells them, there must be something
you can do, the flower beds, the leaves, the hedges need trimming.
She brings the boys powdered donuts, and her parakeet hops
and sings an old jig, for it wasn't often they got company.
"My, my," she thinks, "that one boy is quite the charmer."
It had been years since anyone had complimented her
on the bun of silver hair she still brushed a hundred strokes.
And flowers, the boy knew them, his fast hands bending
around the words for poppies, and bleeding hearts, the vase
of iris on the mantle. She thinks, Lordy, the heat is something,
seems to wear a body down. That's the way they pass the time
in an old house with the shades drawn down, until the boys rise
and start beating her. The fresh faced one signing that he is Satan.
Signing, "Where is the money, bitch, and where are the jewels."
Now her rolls of nylons are gathering blood,
and her breast scar is throbbing, gleaming in the dusty light.
All the time her fingers are moving in the half darkness,
"Please help me, Lord," and the Lord brushes an angel
off his chest, glances down and puts one more breath inside her.
Primes her heart with the living Holy Spirit.
Gets her into a room that overlooks a parking lot,
where every morning, a perky little aid comes in to raise the shades,
rattling on about how the sun can heal most anything that ails us.

Speaking Louder

Not that I blame you, boy, but I can hardly get you
on the phone anymore. I know you're thinking
that gang of little reapers you hang with, hoods up,
Celtic tattooed arms drawn inside your sleeves,
the whole bearing against bearing whir of skateboards
is a spike in the heart of this cold immovable world.
And sure, when you guys fly past, we flinch, shake our heads
and remember what we want from our own romance with youth.
Like my father raising his silver whiskey flask
the night Dorsey's clarinet called them off to war,
the Chinese lanterns above Air Devil's beer garden swaying
to the first sip he nailed in his coffin. And me, you know
I've had my problems with hope, but that's not why I called,
not at all, Son. What I really wanted to say is how much I miss you.
That I have loved you since the first night
your mother's bitch cat wailed in the bushes
as the midwife chanted and pulled you into the candlelight.
How for weeks I slurred your name in all the bars.
How I loved you through all those Sunday mornings
you had to wait by the garret window as the happy families
drove home from church. But above all, I hope you remember
the night we went camping along the banks of Otter Creek,
where those pine needles felt like velvet under our sleeping bags,
as the Coleman lantern hung our shadows in the trees
and a buttery moon broke through the fast clouds.
That's the whole deal, I think. The whole ball of wax,
like your grandpa used to say, his hands arched around an idea.
Just our lonely little planet spinning out of control.
You leaning into me, smelling like Cedar and Dinty Moore,
while I tried vainly to name the constellations.
All the easy ones first, The Big Dipper, the little one,
a few mis-named satellites, as you fell fast asleep in my arms.

Playboys

The Summer of Love when *Time Magazine* said God was dead,
my gung ho father gave up the ghost, too.
Grew a feathery blond mustache, and took to wearing
the turquoise and silver choker I had given him last Christmas.
And on weekends, he'd take his Swedish girlfriend
up river on his boat, the mahogany deck, the cooler of rib-eyes
the pinch of reefer he smoked in his pipe like Hefner,
the Swedish girlfriend's breasts, the whole kit and caboodle,
vibrating with two hundred belching horses of Evinrude
he whipped up river to his new hipster buddies.
But on those days the Swedish babe was home rolling meatballs
for her own Swedish family, I would ride to the island
with my dad, the dirty, choppy river going past the portals
of the cabin where I sat in the dark reading Hesse or Alan Watts.
I was always preparing for the contemplative life then,
a life far above this world of silly men in tight trunks
and aviator glasses, hooting and hollering at every girl
that skied past the beach in a day-glow bikini.
Far above these salesmen's bellies pouring over their waistbands,
six-packs cooling on anchor lines thirty feet down in the river.
Beyond those trick knees and aching shoulders they swung
in slow painful windmills all afternoon, well into their drunks.
Thirty years later, I am no longer so disgusted with this worldly life.
In fact, I remember those girls now, like psychedelic Venuses,
the rainbow wake of their skis fanning out in rooster tails.
The hairless stomachs, the water pouring off in sparkling rivulets,
nothing in their sweet bodies quite sharp or defined yet,
just the unbelievable possibilities of my own hunger.
Say like thin pink medallions of milk fed veal,
or shaved black truffles, or sweetbreads in puff pastry,
strawberries in double cream, and chocolate Grand Mariner tortes.
Like forty something, rounding with the field into the final stretch.

Clean and Sober

I miss you terribly today.
The rainy day embrace of codeine,
the tingle of speed on the hairs of my neck.
I miss the whiskey seeking all the coves
of my arms and feet and eyes.
I miss you, Dad.
No matter how many sips of beer you took
or decks of cards you shuffled at the kitchen table,
they can never equal the times I think of you.
So Happy Father's Day.
Happy days to the winging of balls in leather gloves.
Happy days to big hands tucking a boy in.
I miss you.
You, the blood of my blood.
The cells that wander like beggars through my brain.
The revolutions of truck wheels that drove
over my heart.
And now that I am clean and sober,
where do I find that spot, Dad.
That place I haven't covered up yet
with car wrecks and wives and voices in my head.
Where is that place.
That basement room,
that under the stairs closet,
that tiny cool place I can curl up inside.

A Day At The Circus

When my ex was nine,
her, daddy whom they only saw once a month or so,
took all three sisters to the Berlin Circus.
And all the way there, the girls nearly skipped
out of their bodies to be with their handsome father.
Trying, as they sat on the wooden bleachers lathering
Nutella on a basket of rolls, to remember everything;
the colors, the balloons floating up like jellyfish,
the silly clowns spraying spritzer in their big white mouths,
A little something to fall back on when he was gone.
And her handsome ruddy father who sat one row down
just couldn't keep his eyes off the prancing ponies
in ostrich feathers, or the girl who balanced on top,
the flame of her hair like a birthday candle,
when this other man, this quick man who sat behind my ex,
began to sweat among all those blue pleated skirts.
Began to think that every man's worm should have its turn.
So he grabbed my ex's hand and while her daddy prayed
for moral guidance as the trapeze girl went swinging
hot inside his brain, this other man spilled his seed
into my ex's palm, and disappeared into the foggy light.
She told me she half expected the birds to be weeping
when they walked out into the steel blue day.
Thought the stupid sparrows would be awash in tears.

But birds don't cry, my little flower. They might coo
and prattle in the eaves, but they never, ever cry.
Because if they did, they'd have to cry for Lisa in her basement,
Mother upstairs while the big boys held her down.
And they'd have to weep for my Susie, uncle scrunched
against her in the bowling alley parking lot, neon pins blinking
and falling on her dimpled thighs. And if birds cried,
then there would have to be floods and endless drowning,

water raging through the trailer parks, over the picket fences
and swing sets on our street. It would be so damn biblical.
Every field laid barren and ridged high as a man with salt.

Before The Sun Hangs Itself

While his family sleeps, a man wakes early, goes out to the kitchen to make his coffee, then to the porch where he sits in the dark. The man is so happy to be sitting all alone, so content with his hand wrapped around his hot coffee, that he makes a special, secret pact with himself. That from now on, no matter what happens, he promises to think of nothing else but joy. And to make sure that he is really happy, he reaches up to touch the slab of his tongue that just yesterday had made his family cower. But true to this newfound felicity and bliss, his tongue is as light as a simple children's song and rises happily to the roof of his mouth. Then he looks for the furious gaping holes that once had dotted the walls of his house, but all of them are patched and painted cream. The man is so happy that he begins to wonder how in the world his life could have ever been all these other things. How could he have mistaken the door he tore off its hinges for anything but a door swinging to and fro in the breeze. The man thinks that there is nothing but joy. That even the children from the blind school who pass in front of him on his way to work, even they must be joyful in their own tender ways as they raise their faces up towards heaven. And now, the happy man can barely wait for his son to rise and stumble sleepy and low-lidded to his lap. "Then I will take him in my happy arms," he thinks. "Run my hands the length of this body, tell him of all things holy in this world." A happy man sits on his porch this morning, in love with all this easy, joyful thinking.

Vein

That night in bed, he chewed on the salty blood grit from his hair
and thought how the vein in his father's temple pulsed just like
that cartoon boiler he'd seen last week on *Bugs Bunny*,
the metal plates bulging, the rivets popping out one by one.
And how he wished he could be just like Bugs, not a care in the world
when everybody for miles around knew the whole thing was gonna blow.
Even his dogs knew, nails clicking on the floor, chasing each other
in a heel nipping blur that should have been hilarious,
should've had the whole family sick and dizzy with laughter.
But just like Elmer Fudd, he always stuttered when the piston
of his father's fist came down and his legs wouldn't smoke
or spin, and he couldn't bend into any of those accordion shapes
when his head flew back and broke through the plaster wall.
And he was so dumb that when his father came in later
to stroke his hair and promise that in the morning he would
fix them his famous biscuits and gravy he thought, just maybe,
maybe this time. Because he loved his father's biscuits and gravy,
loved the cast iron skillet and the sizzle of sausage, loved the melted pools
of butter in the center of the flaky dough, and like little Elmer
in his hunting cap, finger to his lips, whispering by the burrow door,
he couldn't fathom how many biscuits, or gallons of gravy, were still to come.

The Famous Writers School

Waking from one of those dreams so close to me I can taste it, I go out on the
porch of the famous writers school to smoke a cigarette, to pretend it isn't
twenty below zero and that I'm not the only idiot out here at this ungodly hour,
my lung hairs freezing, burn holes in my mittens smelling like an incinerated
goat. The only other person awake is the security guard, who at the first glow
of my cigarette, slips on his dripping boots, pats for the half pint in his pocket,
cinches up his gun and trudges over through the snow. He is my man when it
comes to the skinny on which poets were crying in the phone booth tonight,
or which ones he saw stumbling up college hill from the biker bar in town.
But tonight he wants to talk about his fourteen year old daughter who left
last week with some punk. He tells me she left without a word of goodbye,
not even a kiss. And while he's telling me all this, I start thinking about the
wonders of poetry. How it can apply to almost every situation. That if he could
write like all the sleeping poets around us, he could certainly purge himself of
this grief. He could use metaphors for snow to describe it, "My heart is more
hollow than the flagpole that clangs in this blizzard." I tell him he should get
one of those art birds we all carry in our pockets. I tell him, if he had one now,
it would sing, "Her silver studded tongue was so swollen with anger" or "she
left me alone like Ethan Frome, downing long necks by the glow of whale
light." Yes, the art bird with its screws and perfect rainbow warble that makes
the girls tremble, that's what you need, my friend. But hell, he is more country
than even this token southern poet, and they'd probably give him one of those
cheap knockoffs from Taiwan, all clanky and leaking oil. I show him how the
one they gave me for a pocket full of cash won't move without a shove, how it
just sits there most of the time like a stupid-ass turkey. But instead of dwelling
on that, we take a couple of swigs from his bottle and go out into the quad
where we start flapping our arms and making whisky angels in the snow. To
the left of us are the shrouded White Mountains, and to the right, the rooms of
suicidal girls, thin poems burning on the window sills. And behind us are the
teachers, powder kegs of liquor wafting above their beds. The guard and I look
at each other. We are as still now as death. Then we lift our heads back and let
the snow pour down our throats. I speak in tongues for this friend of mine and
his daughter, and all these sweet flakes of God's design that have brought us

together. This convergence of prophets, this body of scribes and raconteurs, that all together might make one moment of difference on this pockmarked world that neither awaits us nor cares which of us soars or which of us drowns, sitting in this Vermont blizzard,with our mouths wide open.

More From The Brain Diary

After the family was asleep, I took my brain out again, and put it on the bedside table next to the blue lamp and my copy of *The Best American Poetry of 1995*. It seemed to like the air, seemed relieved from those dutiful, crackling passages to the body. With its heaviness cradled in my gaze, I watched the ghosts and black faced letters climbing up the gray ridges, looking for a place to escape. And there on one spongy side were my common deceits ready at any moment to fall at the feet of this woman I love. Up near the top were the pearls of my children sleeping by the road of their journeys eastward, skin a swirling pink of goodness and light. The rest of my brain had not changed. The whole of it was still made of churning, murky parts. There were the obligatory crows, of course, and a fault line crisscrossed with the white slats of a crib, drenched in the salt that reflected a boy's yearning. There was a cave. There was a covered bridge whose pinhole of light opened onto all the plans I had abandoned and taken up again. As always, here was that postage sized spot where I create my life. The small stone house on a cliff above the sea. And down in the surf were all the people I had deceived into loving me. They could barely walk. It was like they were under some incredible weight that made them hunch over, drag their heads in an ugly and frail manner as if waiting for death. I could see that I was still Lord of the Sun there. That each of my subjects wore a mask I had forged with tin and pasted on moss. All day long I beat on the masks in my workshop behind the house on the cliff. I would fashion boulders with chicken wire and gravel for them to carry around their necks. I would build clumsy wings from dead gulls found rolling in the surf. I cannot stop. I am obsessed, apparently, with making them in my image. One shelf in my workshop is filled with voice boxes, another with attitudes, and another with desire for me. But the ones on the beach dragging along the sand confuse me. Experiments gone bad? Weak malcontents? Who would dare pull at the buckles of wings that I have fashioned so beautifully? I am obviously the only light in this postage sized moonscape. It is apparent that I am a god here. A god without subjects that will bow down to me. So, I must sleep now and hope that soon my simple children will come to their senses. I must sleep, then rise to scour the beach for more glazed adornments. For more artifacts that will make them love and worship me.

As A Man Thinks

If your man ever starts wandering again, running from anguish
to anguish, nose to the ground for any fresh cut bloom,
its rosy dew still dripping – then take him into the center of you.
That old familiar haunt where he can come and go,
drift in on the surf to that sun baked house with all the things
men like him feel they deserve; the shelves of accolades,
and berry brown girls whispering his poems on gauze covered beds.
Do all this, then slip from his thighs while he sleeps
and tie him to the bed with strands of silk. Take the largest
needle you can find from your grandmother's sewing box
and heat it on the burner of the stove until it is white with your desire.
Then like the market vendors used to do, to make their sea hued
love birds sing more sweetly of earth's invisible graces,
pierce both his eyes through your reflection and down to the nerve.
I know. I know. He will scream himself awake, and there will be weeks
of fevers and hallucinations, months of unbearable sobbing.
But ignore these, cool his brow, salve the blisters and yellow crusting.
Whisper once a day, I understand your heartache, love.
Put him by the window with the ringed wedding quilt across his lap,
until that one morning when you will enter, breaking the beam
of light that warms his face, and he will finally cock his proud head
and turn in your direction, grateful at last for all he has,
breaking into the sweetest aria you could ever hope to hear.

Fire

The true names of three family members who perished in a local fire

My left arm is withered from where I tried to get Faith.
The flames roared like a train and the glass cracked
and the walls bled down. I have never felt such pain.
My mom named me Hope. Dad says they never had a chance
and not to blame myself. Dad says Mom loved us all.
Faith's princess doll melted in her hands. The fireman said
Destiny never even woke up. We got more flowers
than you could believe, Teddy Bears and ribbons all along our fence.
I got a new bike, but it's broken now, and everyone forgets.
I think Dad hates my name. He calls me Pumpkin,
Sweetheart, anything but Hope. I hope he doesn't hate me.
But I'm not sure of anything much. Except sometimes at night,
I think I hear Faith and Destiny in the next room.
They are giggling and laughing at some silly joke like little sisters do.
A high pitched laugh, that used to make Mom and me roll our eyes,
like it was going to drive us crazy unless they stopped.

Amends

I thought I'd bring her flowers,
Tulips maybe and a baguette of crusty bread.
Some cheeses and body oil
for when the kids went down to sleep.
But I got tore up instead.
Shit faced, falling down, in my cups,
singing to nobody, stumbling drunk.
I thought I'd save up a month's salary,
pile all the kids in the car.
Leave while it was dark and head down
to Disney World, singing all the way.
But I stayed out all night and spent my check
at the Oriental spa, had to turn my pockets
inside out for change to pay the cab.
If good intentions were kisses
I'd be drowning in slobber. If promises
were gold, I'd be old man Midas.
But my wife irons clothes instead,
resells them at yard sales, and the kids
buy Happy Meals, look through the cheap
little viewfinders at scenes from the Magic Kingdom.
And I do just about what the hell I want.
Complain when things aren't just so.
A crumb on the floor, a bowl of soggy cereal.
Anything can set me off and running,
to something irreversible, something unforgivable.
Something for them to remember me by.
Something in their throats, no matter how you tell the story.

Reincarnation

I just bought an old fixer-upper down in Portland,
near the bend of the river where I was born,
near a quick mart that I went into a few days ago
and listened to an old drunk biker ranting
how "we ought to shoot every one of them niggers!"
And being in the middle of reading the *Tibetan
Book of the Dead* again, I wanted to take the old biker's
leathery hand and say, "Brother, this is all illusion,
those burning streets you once flew down,
my mother being raped on the rusted flotsam
behind the canal, the blinking red-green lights
on the endless barges, the campsites under the bridge,
all of it will be judged in the end, so be ready,
clear your heart, make room for infinite love."
But my bones are fragile from falling on asphalt,
and all I can manage is a look like "I could kill you, too."
Then I walk home to my old clapboard house,
to the neighbor's sleek brown pit bull throwing itself
against the fence. I go inside to the moldy walls,
to the dead things in the attic I'm afraid to clean out.
My mother has been moldy twelve years now,
the shell of her soul in a grave that I dream
of digging up sometimes, tearing the wet wood apart
for a lock of hair, a jaw bone, a gold plated earring,
something that would finally sing me to sleep.
And I look for my father in the wind-beaten faces
of the old men I pass, draped in crooked doorways,
nodding like they've known me for a lifetime,
probably thinking behind those tired, wry grins,
that it's almost over, bags packed, tickets bought.
And maybe the light of love will carry them on,
but me, I've wanted and wasted and let anger lead me
so much, that even a fool can tell I'll be coming back.

Funeral

I've been down in that basement full of cherry caskets
lined up like a used car lot, these faux bookcases,
guardian vaults, scentless flowers, perpetual care,
all the hidden guilty charges they get us for.
In the back room my neighbor's friends are gathered
by the buffet, swigging beers and punctuating
with carrot sticks the life of his small escapades.
But then I saw his dervish of a little girl.
She was weaving in and out of the freshly shaved legs,
in and out of the stifled sobs and game time yawns.
She was coming closer and closer to the casket,
but no one seemed to notice. Then she cleared
the flowers and pictures of him as a rouge cheeked boy
and with one spectacular leap she cleared the railing
to scramble up beside him on the satin pillow.
She kept saying, "A kiss goodnight, a kiss goodnight!"
I'd like to think that if the soul's feather really does drift on,
or if we can look down upon them, like it's said,
that he would have told her how pretty she was today,
and how much his up-folded arms reminded him
of that Christmas morning when he carried her down the hall.
And how he hadn't know then, hadn't realized once
among the lights and toys, that his arms, death's arms,
these frail and skinny arms I watched her lean on,
were as full that morning as they would ever be again.

The Last One

The summer I was eighteen and the only virgin left on earth,
my buddy Richard and I would smoke a fat one on the way to work
and scarf down a dozen donuts before the foreman started in on us,
calling us "you girls" and going on all day about his little hotty of a girlfriend
who'd come by every day for lunch, disappearing into his trailer
while we'd sit there eating Big Macs, watching for any sign of its rocking.
And yeah, I thought I saw you today. I'm almost sure that was you,
minus the midriff sweater in the dead heat of summer, minus the
Olds Cutlass, and the six pack of sweating beer you'd bring every day.
I'm sure that was you behind the counter at Walgreeens, painting blush
on some deserving rag of a housewife, her two kids pulling at every seam.
You know, almost every night that summer I'd get a twelve pack,
and put it right beside me like a real girlfriend and drive out into the country.
Drive past the tiger lily ditches, past the blue corn flowers,
past the rabbits darting in front of me, past the mailboxes I'd rise up
and hit with beer cans so they reverberated. Half blind, I'd imagine
you'd told the foreman to kiss your ass and were here right beside me,
long eyelashes fluttering against my neck, feeling your tongue work
its way down to my lap. Yeah sweetie, I'm sure that was you today.
A little too much rouge, a little too much living on the edge where we both
have balanced since that summer, thinking we're still driving out in the country.
Still dodging the hearts of roadside oaks, my foot stomping through
to the core of our hot young lives. Like we would never be bored,
never catch ourselves working or shopping in a place like this.

At Eleven Before Becoming Fully Human

The other night, I was watching the original 'Bride of Frankenstein' with my son,
the part right before the hunters careen in and torch the quaint little hut.
The part where the monster and the old blind man are sitting by the fire
as the old man plays Ave Maria on his violin, and the monster grows sleepy,
warmed by the wine and the first hint of peace in his short, troubled life.
I look over at my son to see if thinks this old black and white is too sappy.
He turns away when I look, tears streaming down his face, just as the monster
is learning to say, Good....Lonely....Heart.....Friend. And then the hunters come,
lay waste to the hut, drag the old man away, and the monster is waving
his arms all crazy like, roaring as the flames start to lick at him.
And my ten year old son is looking away, as if he is burning himself.
As if he is the one forsaken. Engulfed in the enormity of all our sins.

The Fifth Of July

Boys run the confetti streets,
Salvaged cherry bombs boom low in the heat.
The front page news is Mushroom clouds
And tethered sheep skinned alive.
Hospital fans whir and suck in the city soot.
I am still my mother's sweet magnolia blossom,
Petal upon petal folded in on itself.
She is calling out again, Keep him safe.
I smell ammonia and bright lights.
Spines are dulled and wolves in high heels
And blue suits gather in the wings.
The intern clamps the forceps, dents the skull again.
My bastard life begins, cockeyed at her breast.

My Neon Girl

Three years before I was born, my momma would sit at home
reading her movie magazines and curling her fly-away hair,
while she waited for my grandma to come in late and lie down beside her.
More times than not, my grandma would smell like a mix
of White Shoulders and Jim Beam when she'd snuggle up
and say, "What you gonna do, Pumpkin, just let a good man like that go?"
In the morning they'd fry up the steaks he'd brought my grandma,
and they'd put the roses in a clean jelly jar on the window sill.
My grandma would tell her how she'd lick the salt off her lover's neck.
How you folded a man's pants and steamed them in the shower
so his wife wouldn't smell a thing when he got home.
Or the way you could lie there all night listening to the hum
of that neon girl outside of Collier's Motor Court.
The green shadow of her on the drapes, completely unfazed by the concrete,
making one perfect dive after another into the parking lot.

Crib

My rust colored grandpa comes in,
Hangs his hat on the hook
And cracks open his lips
That have barely spoken all day.
A train whistle turns his head.
Must be Tom on the 5:45,
And then he calls out.
"Anna Lee, you come on down, girl,
and cook us up some supper."
His tired footsteps up the stairs.
"Oh lord. What's that girl gone and done?"
I feel him coming over to the crib,
He winces at the smell,
Throws the stocking nipple of sugar water
Clear across the room, takes me
Downstairs and fixes a bottle.
Drips the milk on his liver spotted wrist.
A burnt sweetness from the caramel factory
Drifts in from the kitchen window.
My heart is beating like a hummingbird's
As I listen for her footsteps.

Bobby

Later that night, they clung to each other
On the dance floor, beer garden lanterns
Swaying above Bear Grass Creek
That flowed past the Stock Yards.
She thought, I have never met a man
Whose brain moved this fast.
It must have been the five long-necks talking,
Whatever covered up the metal taste
Of his kisses, covered up the ghost songs
Of butcher's wives, knee deep in the water,
Skimming tallow off the bloody creek.

Spiraling

It was near dawn
When my grandma and Bobby
Rode across the creek bed and parked.
The red tailed hawks and buzzards
Already spiraling in the mist.
Sweat was pouring down the inside
Of Bobby's windshield, the headlights
Barely stretching to the river.
It was like Paradise to my grandma.
The ache leaving her waitress feet.
The beer calming whatever fears
Rose up with Bobby's cock.
Her hand filled with its promise,
The viens and tributaries,
Unknown currents churning through it.

Twitching

Junior Hadley woke in darkness,
Put his coffee and eggshells on to boil,
Then tiptoed down to the barn
Where his first drink was hidden in the hay.
It was spider webs and dew like every morning.
Hi pointer lay under the tack bench,
Full of cockles and burrs.
A weak watted bulb bathed the cows
And the Morgan shuffled and snorted in its stall.
Junior called his dog, who slinked towards him,
Growling, slobbering, haunches flat and bobtail twitching,
My grandmother's femur bone locked in his jaws.

Chrome Blind Love

Here I go, thinking out of turn again,
when I got about a million things to do.
How I've made up all these crazy stories
about Momma and you for my selfish bidding.
Call it what you will, why my dumb head
keeps thinking it knows anything at all.
Why at any truck stop I start looking for you,
and then before I know it, that jukebox twang
is calling to me from way up in your cab.
"Hop on up boy, we got to drive like mad tonight.
Got to rattle over all the knobs and rusty bridges
with Billy loves Amber scrawled on the side.
Yeah son, we're gonna wake all the fishes
from their summer longing, count every silt filled tire
that blooms along the riverbank."
So I must be thinking out of turn again,
that just because I've got a few sparrows loving me,
sweet smelling heads against my chest,
a man doesn't need his past.
Or just because I've never seen you, Dad,
you aren't out there passing some wet-dry county line,
shifting down around a blind man's curve,
horn bellowing, amphetamine eyes glowing in the dark.
And I must be a real smart-ass to boot,
seeing you pull into that parking lot where Momma
waited at the bar, her cotton shift clinging sweaty
to the last few rolls of baby fat you loved to grab.
By then, everything was tangled up in you.
The high noon sun melting the asphalt down,
oil belching rigs grinding and blinding each other
with chrome bumpers and confederate mud flaps.
And poor Momma, half drunk, keeps licking her fingers
until last week's taste of you seeps up in her pores

trying her best to name the rhythm of your hips,
what to call her head banging on the side door,
silver belt buckle cutting curlicues into her thighs,
fiddle and woe songs turned up loud on the radio.
I'll tell you, there's no reason not to come back.
I'm probably a chip off the old block,
swaddled up in my petty life like you must've been.
And hell, if that don't do it, I just bought a 68 Ford pick-up
that some old farmer had. It's black as a lawyers heart,
with an oak rail bed. It's the bomb, Daddy.
So cherry, you just got to see it for yourself.

Conception, 1953

Way out on Dixie Highway, across the street
from where the Voice of Thunder Apostolic Congregation
would sing the praises of a forgiving Lord
less than eight hours from now, Jerome Shipley looked out
the kitchen window of Shipley's Diner to where my father,
whom I never met, sat swaying drunk in one of the booths,
trying to stick his sloppy tongue into my mother's ear,
as Jerome whispered to himself, "Fuck the red faced jackass,
thinking he looks all slick in his Dress Khakis,"
as he flipped my father's six oz. breakfast steak,
brushed some half rancid butter on top of it,
and pressed the spatula down hard to break the stringy membranes,
and with one hand, cracked three eggs on the griddle,
poured four ladles of batter, and looked out again
to make sure no one was looking, and just as the Wurlitizer
clicked down the fourth in six cuts of a Hank Williams tune,
Jerome worked up a hocker from the bulge of Red Man
in his cheek and let a long strand of it drop down
into the middle of my father's buttermilk pancakes,
and then slammed his palm down hard on the bell,
choking off its ring, and yelled, "Order Up!"
startling my mother, whose hand was fluttering
under the table, only a hair above my father's pants.

Attached

The boy with the long hair and leather fringed jacket
who used to sit in the woods behind his school
watching the way the sun hit the passing stream,
while he read *Siddhartha,* and wrote love poems
that tore at his insides with so much beauty
he could barely give them to the girls in question,
opens the paper today to the pictures of a dark-
skinned boy with wires attached to his genitals,
and later he finds himself standing at a giant
hardware store, debating the merits of a gas powered
grass trimmer as opposed to the electric one,
and though it seems like a small gesture, he buys
the electric one, and when he gets back into his car
there is a moth caught between the dashboard and window,
so he cups it gently in his hand, slips it out into the air
to watch it flap madly across the giant parking lot
filled to the brim with trucks and cars that make us brave
and sure of ourselves as we drive on to the next century,
each of our wallets filled with pictures of our children,
of our grandchildren, and each of us loving something,
be it pain, or be it the new Tudor houses in the cottonwoods'
ghostly light, by the memory of a creek where he used to sit,
or be it not quite enough to change the cry of that boy,
some mother's son with electric wires attached to his genitals,
or the splash of the chlorophyll against the fishing line
of his trimmer as it spins into this universe he has built.

Bruises

And you were thinking what,
as you flew through the first November snow?
Of ice chips on her lips or accordion straws?
That if you were lucky, you could catch
that last crumb of light before it flew
from her eyes to beat against the window?
Oh my children, my fevered ones,
what did you expect? A vein of love,
a bed of bruises and cataracts to fall into
as the paddles arched her off the bed,
flopped her down until the line was flat?
And did you pray that some hooded
oarsman would rub his salve around her heart,
heal the loneliness that killed her slowly?
But then the nurse walked into the room.
Let her flaming ringlets of hair
brush against your cheek, her starched blouse
in pointed sympathy for this old story.
Did you foresee her number hard and fast
in your pocket as you walked past the droning
promises, and prayers, into the night?
Were you caught dreaming of the nurse again?
Did you check your hair in the mirror,
clean a bit of yellow from your bloodshot eyes?
Did you drive past field after field of frozen stubble,
past night lights glowing around children's beds?
Did you see all the sons and daughters sleeping.
So close to love, they could wake and bang
against their parents' wall any time they wanted,
any time they felt themselves going under fast?
Did you want to sit up and call out – like that?

In The Cool White Hum Of Summer Nights

Sometime near the middle of June,
I'd help my dad lug up the air-conditioner
from the corner of the basement,
he taking the big end, the compressor,
heavy as a miniature ice factory,
full of spiders we'd hose off in the yard,
then lift it up to the living room window
and plug it in for the sweet sound of it
all summer long, and one by one,
we shut our houses up, some with ones
like we had, and some with central air,
and all of us became real quiet when summer
rolled around, maybe the faint smell
of lighter fluid, a dog or two barking,
a siren, or the cry of a child when you passed,
maybe a blue flicker from the shades,
but all in all, dead quiet, like up and down
the manicured suburban streets,
with the tee-tee-tee of sprinklers on the lawns,
and the big cars squeezed in side by side,
only happy, contented people must've lived there,
that something so serene and still at dusk,
must've meant only kind things were said
to each other, and that all the children
were touched with such love and tenderness,
they would fall fast asleep without jerking,
without listening hour after hour,
like someone crouched in the back of a cave,
for any sound that seemed out of place.

Goodbye For Now

This is for the Alcohol.
Old friend that loved me first, comforted me, divorced me,
charged me, sentenced me, with the murder of my spirit,
made me do those things to you.
This is for the Inhalants.
That goofy paint thinner smile. The helicopters landing in my head,
that whoosh of fire raining down. The cells you never will return.
This is for the Coke and Speed.
Tingling every little hair and making me the center of the universe.
The way I could smell you in a crowd.
Give me another line and I'll explain it all.

This is for the Needle.
The rite of passage, the bridges we almost burned.
The clichéd belt and blood, the way we fell and fell.
Lost at sea in a tortoise shell, made just for you and me.
This is for the PCP.
The tunnels you collapsed. The pinpoints of light. The rings of Hell.
This is for the Codeine.
Best friend of my lover, Alcohol, warming me by your fire.
Even through the bones I broke trying to get back to you,
tender was your embrace, the leaving so damned difficult.
This is for the Herb.
Your pipe and rolling rituals. Your sweet brownies.
Your whispering through the common hours.
Your smile when the world goes flat and the way
you let me laugh, and do nothing, nothing, nothing.

This is for the Cigarettes,
I miss you the most. Dream about you. My lungs ache
just remembering how you used to fill me up.
How you made a hard day good again, and for your kiss,
I'd go crawling through the garbage. Sincerely, your slave.

This is for all of you bastards
that never stop calling, that come over in the middle of the night,
whining about this, about how you need me, miss me, got to have me now.
Listen. I can't afford the company, can't trust you like I did.
But give me a moment's notice that I'm checking out,
and I swear, we'll have a great big party, invite every friend we know.

Muse

You are my troubled harbor where the green ships limp in.
You are full of splintered planks and slick weed docks,
whores in jade and blue veined breasts sagging way down.
You are the broken mast, and the bloody harpoon boat,
the sparkling gold dust floor at the fat man's lending house.
All the barnacles and the beaten, bloody Albatross.
You are the crow's nest, the rummy eyes, a starving monkey
spitting on the blind man's shoulder, the salt in every wound.
You mean nothing to me, you were never on my lips.
No gust of you wafting orchids from the jungle's rotting steam.
You are a case of guns. You are the worst of my rotted teeth.
You are the hardness in my liver. You are the calcium grinding
in my shoulder. You are the shadows that hummed at the soft
spot in my brain, telling me to love you. You are a dead dog
washed up on the beach, all its bulging and eyes filmed over,
putrid gases escaping downwind. You are this rainy day,
with its cold dripping birds folded in. The fallen nest outside,
the eggs splattered and yolks sucked up by the Bandit Jays.
You are my useless friend, staying for months in the basement.
Giving me nothing but grief. No work, no money, pissing in the drain.
The answer, the depth of you, the bottle hidden whenever I come down.

I Love The Fair Because It Makes Me Look Skinny

Makes me want to let myself go,
stumble through the miles of ill conceived quilts,
past the swaggering horses in their appointed tents,
the braided girls, and the looks of their Mexican help.
I love the fair, the red, sweaty faces of the hungover carnies,
the loose bolts on the Tilt-A-Whirl,
the way deep down we must really trust each other.
I love the sleeping cows and the sleeping cowboys,
the straw bales and the piles of shit,
and the slim chance that I'll have to talk about poetry.
I love the fair, the oval rims and the rubber balls,
the darts, the softballs never landing in their peach baskets.
I love the young new loves made and lost in a week,
the sorghum, honey, pork butt, country ham, deep fried Twinkie,
elephant ear, whipped pineapple, mix of smells.
I love my wife and children just a little bit more
high up on the Ferris wheel and the giant swing.
I love the way money means nothing and flies from your hands,
dads holding kids they hardly ever see,
reaching down and spending more than they have,
and glad-happy to do it, again and again.
I love the impatient woman in front of me,
who's come all the way from Hawesville for the free mammogram,
cancer screening, eye test, and five minute massage.
I love being taken, made a fool of, challenged to win a crinkly stuffed frog,
the seams so lightly sewn we'll be lucky to get it home.
I love all the tractors, carts, cars, trucks, pens, whirring oiled machines
that keep it going, all the millions of light bulbs blinking and glaring
onto one big shining stew of what's left of America.
All of us equal, shoulder to shoulder, breast to breast, wrinkle to wrinkle,
roll of fat to fat, hope to hope, poverty to poverty,
cheap hats and sunglasses, and waddling smiles where ever you look.

Is That You

Back in the day, when I was tripping every chance I got,
sheets of blotter, micro-dot, orange barrel, window pane,
Mr. Natural, coursing through my veins, illuminating
the glorious fluid of life, the way I sometimes couldn't even see
my parents when I got home, only a bitter looking aura,
a smell of sulfur blocking the way to my box of lights and shadow,
and my Border Collie, who would look so concerned,
never let his Saint Francis eyes leave me while I held on,
and then before I even thought it, he'd jump down from my bed,
turn away while I masturbated, all the way to the end of a rainbow
splashing through the darkness with Mary Shepherd's face
bobbing in the briny waves of it and through the currents
in the darkness and through my eyelids that closed tight
and were faint protection when the scaries finally came,
the spiders and backless swarms of passing nightmares swept
by me like Dorothy looking out her Kansas window, and the sounds
that the mice could only hear, the furnace in love with its blue gas,
and the pipes aching in their iron throats for water
and the hermit crabs digging, each grain of sand a boulder,
and even through all that, in case they came back with ice cubes tinkling
to ask about my day, I could still pull it together just in time
to hold those inane conversations that thirty odd years later
I still have on a daily basis with daily people, because I'm so nice,
or want to be loved, or maybe because we are social animals
scratching out our bearings, afraid to be alone, but it's on automatic,
Brother, its all the same, knock me on the noggin, and I can still talk
about the storm, shake my head, and that accident where the girl
was thrown from her car, what a shame, what a shame,
even when I can't see you standing there, and all of me is gone,
my mouth still mentioning your wife, or how the kids are,
and if the flesh is falling off of you, if your skin is turning to rubber

or you're melting away into the oily pavement, forgive me for not noticing,
but what a lovely day, and the humidity is lower than it's been in weeks,
and maybe we'll get a little rain, the crops, the grass is suffering,
all that debris, same routine, same routine, here you come, I'm smiling now.

Levity

They never laughed much, except when all three of them
had hit on some magical equation of scotch or bourbon
that made them raw and tender as newborn babies,
without a memory of what they had ever done to each other.
Or sometimes it happened at Christmas when baby Jesus
would wash the house clean with twisted pine and bayberry,
and they would laugh with such an urgency that the dogs
would run from the strange lightness bleeding from their eyes.
They would be bent double from it, wailing like crazy people
lurching forward and knocking over ashtrays and vases.

Then a light would blow out on the tree, or someone would go
to fix another drink, sure that they could prolong this epiphany.
And all at once, the richness, the unreal spice of it would hit them,
begin to twist and tremble in the pit of their stomachs.
Like when one of the dogs had gulped down a baby rabbit,
they would begin to feel it coming back, feel the bones
ripping up through their stomachs, that toothy head of levity,
squeezing wet and shiny through their unhinged mouths.
Impossible to think they could have ever swallowed it whole.

Rage

My father had it in his throbbing brain when he came home.
Had it in his bloody knuckles that shattered walls and wood.
I could hear it in the way his car pulled in. The crunching tires.
The length of time before the door slammed shut.
My mother had it in her tongue unleashed with scotch
and whipping round the house in every dusty corner.
She was afraid of night. Afraid of what the darkness spoke.
And someone had it when I was a baby. Threw me down the stairs.
The deepness of that scar I've shown the girls for years.
Thinking, now they know and will surely leave me.
Now they see what I can do to them, and only a fool or a child,
or someone in love with pain, would step off into a space like that.
But some must like the danger. Or thinking, like my neighbor
who plowed his little farm right by the river, that they alone
deserve some saving grace. That those who love the most,
are always blessed and can stop the rain from falling.

And You

Imagination is the key to happiness, my mother used to say,
and how much I was like my dad,
how close, it seemed, even though I was adopted,
the fruit had fallen from the tree.
This was long after my parents got over
their disgust for each other,
settled into the happy hours and key parties.
It would be a couple of years
before I found that strange, mechanical rubber face
hidden on a shelf in the basement.
The lips that must have loved him like my mother never had.
The battery operated O of them sucking out
his dreams down in the cement and mold.
Right after that, I cut Miss November's air brushed face
from my dad's *Playboy*,
put her in my Tandy leather wallet to show
the boys on the bus, how beautiful my green-eyed mother was.
And my best friend brought the Moody Blues',
"Nights in White Satin" lyrics scratched out in his notebook,
claiming to have written them himself.
His dad beat him a little, and later that year
he had an affair with my mom, and then one weekend
she flew to Mexico, though she hated Mexicans,
hated their food, and seemed to be worried about her weight.

What The Gods Must Do For Fun

After spending the afternoon at the Lee's, smoking pot
and watching *F Troop, Batman* and *Gilligans Island*,
I came into the house for dinner, just as our Greek
foreign exchange student, who was in love with my mother,
took a cleaver from the kitchen drawer and chased
my dad around the house and back to the bedroom closet
where my dad held the door and reached up on the shelf
to draw his silver 38 police special from its black holster,
and then burst out, waving the gun towards Demetrius,
who was sobbing something about taking my mother
back to Greece, and Dad, who was normally just another drunk
who killed his days down by the river, feigning interest
in barges and old purring Johnson & Johnson motors,
deck patch, and mahogany stain, was suddenly my hero again,
as he backed this little Greek Fucker (no pun intended Mom)
all the way through the house and onto the back porch,
Dad's big ears fiery red, that vein that spelled "heap of trouble"
throbbing in his forehead, as he took aim and said,
"What you gonna do now, asshole," and then Demetrius
somewhere out of the depths of his Greek, bronzed genes,
made one last half-hearted movement, more a lean
than anything else, towards my dad who laid a marker out
right between his eyes, right as we closed ours,
imagining for that split second, all the trouble and inconvenience,
before Dad dropped the barrel down and fired a round
through the hemp rug I'd tried to smoke once, and into the concrete,
and by the time the police arrived, we had all fixed ourselves
a stiff scotch and soda, a happy go lucky family again,
suddenly hungry for each other's company, The Hero,
the Adulteress, and the Wasted Teenager, letting the high
of adrenaline blanch out all of our hatred for a moment,
letting fear stand in for respect, letting Demetrius be carried
away for a few days of observation, and watching them

go, I felt like some movie character, waving awkwardly slow,
while the gangster, hidden behind the door, shakes his head,
runs his finger dramatically across his throat, I felt just like that,
telepathically calling out to them, C o m e   b a c k, C o m e   b a c k.

Just In Time

You came just in time
like Browning at Elizabeth's door,
when her fire had almost died
one ember flickering as he knocked.
You came as light had dimmed
to almost nothing, and nothing moved
except the workhouse of my heart.
You came with racing clouds,
with oily blades of road-side grass,
bitter in their sun drenched taste.
You came to this immigrant from sorrow.
Came to my fifty ragged years,
with Jonquils in the snow, with saplings
and willow waving mossy creeks.
You came with prisms on the violet water,
to eyes that only see some distant death.
You came so I could love myself again.

ACKNOWLEDGMENTS

My thanks to the editors and publishers of the following periodicals, anthologies, and recordings in which some of these poems appeared previous to the publication of this book.

Poets of the New Century (anthology, Godine Books)
    "Speaking Louder"
    "Playboys"
    "Chrome Blind"

PERMAFROST
    "The memory of touch"

Kentucky to Iceland and Beyond (CD)
    "Kentucky Dream Time"

The Literary Renaissance
    "Chrome Blind Love"

Leo Magazine
    "VEGA"

Gargoyle Magazine
    "Playboys"

Arable: a Literary Journal
    "As a Man Thinks"
    "Rage"
    "Air"
    "You Came With Blue Cliches"
    "Road Trip Revision At Fifty"